Mastering the Art of Sales: Strategies and Techniques for Success in a Dynamic World

Written by Samuel Buckiewicz

A thank you to John, Randy, Andy, and Devon. I would not be as successful as I am without you in my career.

Anyone can take these basic steps to become successful in sales!

Table of Contents

Chapter 6: Sales and Marketing Alignment

- Understanding the relationship between sales and marketing
- Strategies for aligning sales and marketing goals
- Building a collaborative relationship between sales and marketing teams
- Developing effective marketing materials to support sales efforts

Chapter 7: Sales Technology and Automation

- The role of technology in sales
- Understanding and leveraging sales automation tools
- Using customer relationship management (CRM) software to drive sales success
- Analyzing sales data to optimize performance

Chapter 8: Continual Learning and Improvement

- The importance of continuous learning and development in sales
- Strategies for ongoing sales training and education
- Staying up-to-date with industry trends and changes
- Developing a growth mindset to drive success in sales

Chapter 9: Conclusion

- Recap of key takeaways for success in sales
- Final thoughts and tips for success in sales
- The future of sales and what it means for sales professionals

Appendix: Additional Resources for Success in Sales

- Recommended books, podcasts, and blogs for sales professionals
- Sales training programs and courses
- Sales conferences and events

EXCLUSIVE PAPERBACK CLOSES AT THE END

Chapter 1: Introduction

Sales is the lifeblood of any business. It is the process of persuading potential customers to purchase products or services that meet their needs or desires. Without sales, businesses cannot generate revenue and ultimately, cannot survive. Therefore, understanding and mastering the art of sales is crucial for anyone who wants to succeed in business.

Success in sales is not just about closing deals or hitting quotas. It's about building relationships, understanding customer needs, and providing solutions that address those needs. Success in sales requires a combination of skills, strategies, and a mindset that is focused on delivering value to customers.

In this book, we will explore the fundamentals of selling, from prospecting and lead generation to closing deals and managing sales teams. We will also examine the role of marketing in sales, the importance of sales technology and automation, and the ongoing learning and development required for success in sales.

But before we dive into the details of sales, it's important to understand the mindset required for success in this field. Sales can be challenging, with rejection and failure being common occurrences. However, successful sales professionals approach these challenges with a positive attitude and a growth mindset. They see every failure as an opportunity to learn and improve, and they persist even in the face of rejection.

So, whether you're a seasoned sales professional or just starting your career in sales, this book will provide you with the tools, strategies, and mindset required to succeed in this dynamic and exciting field. Let's get started!

Chapter 2: The Fundamentals of Selling

Successful sales professionals understand that selling is not just about closing deals, but also about building relationships with prospects and customers. In this chapter, we will explore the fundamentals of selling, including the sales process, effective communication skills, identifying customer needs, and overcoming objections.

Understanding the Sales Process

The sales process is a series of steps that sales professionals follow to move prospects through the sales funnel and ultimately close deals. While the specifics of the sales process can vary depending on the industry and the product or service being sold, the general steps include:

Prospecting: Identifying potential customers who are likely to be interested in your product or service.
Qualifying: Determining if the prospect is a good fit for your product or service.
Needs analysis: Identifying the prospect's needs, pain points, and challenges.
Presenting: Demonstrating how your product or service can solve the prospect's problems.
Handling objections: Addressing any concerns or objections the prospect may have.
Closing: Asking for the sale and finalizing the deal.
Follow-up: Staying in touch with the customer to ensure satisfaction and identify upsell or cross-sell opportunities.

Building Relationships with Prospects and Customers

Building strong relationships with prospects and customers is essential for success in sales. Sales professionals who prioritize relationship building over closing deals tend to have higher customer retention rates and more consistent sales success. Building relationships involves active listening, empathy, and a willingness to understand the customer's needs and goals.

Developing Effective Communication Skills

Effective communication is critical in sales. Sales professionals must be able to communicate the value of their product or service clearly and persuasively, while also listening carefully to the customer's needs and concerns. Effective communication skills include active listening, clear and concise messaging, and adapting communication styles to match the customer's communication preferences.

Identifying Customer Needs and Pain Points

Successful sales professionals take the time to understand their customer's needs and pain points. By identifying the customer's problems, sales professionals can position their product or service as a solution to those problems. Sales professionals should also be aware of their customer's industry, competitors, and market trends to provide targeted solutions.

Overcoming Objections

Objections are a natural part of the sales process. Successful sales professionals view objections as opportunities to provide additional value and build trust with the customer. Effective objection handling involves active listening, addressing the customer's concerns, and providing solutions that alleviate those concerns.

Conclusion

The fundamentals of selling involve understanding the sales process, building relationships with prospects and customers, developing effective communication skills, identifying customer needs and pain points, and overcoming objections. By mastering these fundamentals, sales professionals can build a strong foundation for success in sales.

Chapter 3: Prospecting and Lead Generation

Prospecting and lead generation are the foundation of successful sales. In this chapter, we will explore the strategies and techniques used to identify and attract potential customers, build a pipeline of leads, and ultimately convert those leads into paying customers.

Identifying Your Ideal Customer

Before you begin prospecting, it's important to identify your ideal customer. This involves understanding the demographics, needs, and pain points of your target audience. You can use customer personas, market research, and customer feedback to build a profile of your ideal customer.

Creating a Prospecting Plan

Once you have identified your ideal customer, you can develop a prospecting plan. This plan should include strategies for identifying and reaching out to potential customers, such as:

Referrals: Ask existing customers, partners, and colleagues for referrals to potential customers.
Networking: Attend industry events, conferences, and trade shows to meet potential customers and build relationships.
Cold calling: Reach out to potential customers via phone or email.
Social media: Use social media platforms like LinkedIn to connect with potential customers and build relationships.
Content marketing: Create valuable content that addresses the needs and pain points of your ideal customer, and use this content to attract potential customers to your website.

Qualifying Leads

Not all leads are created equal. Successful sales professionals take the time to qualify leads to ensure they are a good fit for their product or service. Qualification criteria may include factors like budget, decision-making authority, and timeline.

Managing Your Pipeline

Once you have generated a pipeline of leads, it's important to manage that pipeline effectively. This involves tracking leads, prioritizing follow-up, and moving leads through the sales process. Sales automation tools like customer relationship management (CRM) software can help sales professionals manage their pipeline more effectively.

Conclusion

Prospecting and lead generation are essential for success in sales. By identifying your ideal customer, developing a prospecting plan, qualifying leads, and managing your pipeline, you can build a steady stream of potential customers and ultimately convert those leads into paying customers.

Closing sales is the ultimate goal of the sales process. In this chapter, we will explore the techniques and strategies used to close deals and convert prospects into paying customers.

Chapter 4: Closing Sales

Building Rapport and Trust

Before you can close a sale, it's important to build rapport and trust with the prospect. Building rapport involves establishing a connection with the prospect and demonstrating that you understand their needs and goals. Building trust involves demonstrating your expertise, credibility, and integrity.

Using Sales Techniques

Sales professionals use a variety of techniques to move prospects closer to a buying decision. Some common sales techniques include:

Trial closes: Asking questions throughout the sales process to gauge the prospect's interest and commitment.
Assumptive closes: Assuming the sale is already made and asking for final details like payment and delivery.
Urgency closes: Creating a sense of urgency around the buying decision, such as by offering limited-time discounts or promotions.
Objection handling: Addressing any concerns or objections the prospect may have about the product or service.
Value proposition: Reinforcing the value proposition of the product or service and how it will benefit the prospect.

Asking for the Sale

The most important part of closing a sale is asking for the sale. This involves making a clear and direct request for the prospect to make a buying decision. Effective sales professionals use a variety of closing techniques to ask for the sale, such as:

Direct close: Asking the prospect directly if they are ready to make a buying decision.
Alternative close: Offering the prospect a choice between two options, both of which involve making a buying decision.
Assumptive close: Assuming the sale is already made and asking for final details like payment and delivery.

Following Up After the Sale

After closing a sale, it's important to follow up with the customer to ensure their satisfaction and identify opportunities for upselling or cross-selling. Effective follow-up involves providing exceptional customer service, addressing any concerns or issues the customer may have, and identifying additional needs or pain points that the customer may have.

Conclusion

Closing a sale is the ultimate goal of the sales process. By building rapport and trust with the prospect, using effective sales techniques, asking for the sale, and following up after the sale, sales professionals can convert prospects into paying customers and build long-term relationships that lead to repeat business and referrals.

Chapter 5: Managing Sales Teams

Managing a sales team can be a complex and challenging task. In this chapter, we will explore the skills and techniques used to build and manage effective sales teams that achieve their goals and drive business success.

Building a Sales Team

Building a sales team involves identifying the roles and responsibilities needed to achieve your sales goals, hiring the right people for those roles, and creating a team culture that fosters collaboration, growth, and success. Some key steps in building a sales team include:

Defining roles and responsibilities: Clearly define the roles and responsibilities of each team member to ensure that everyone is working towards the same goals.
Hiring the right people: Hire people with the skills, experience, and attitude needed to succeed in the sales roles.
Training and development: Provide ongoing training and development opportunities to help your team members grow and improve their skills.
Creating a team culture: Foster a team culture that promotes collaboration, open communication, and continuous improvement.

Setting Sales Goals and Metrics

Setting sales goals and metrics is a critical part of managing a sales team. Goals provide focus and direction, while metrics help you measure progress and identify areas for improvement. Some common sales metrics include:

Revenue: The amount of revenue generated by the sales team.
Sales volume: The number of units sold by the sales team.
Average deal size: The average value of each sale made by the sales team.
Sales cycle length: The length of time it takes to close a sale.

Motivating and Managing Your Team

Motivating and managing your sales team involves providing the support, resources, and guidance needed to achieve their goals. Some effective techniques for motivating and managing your team include:

Coaching and feedback: Provide regular coaching and feedback to help your team members improve their skills and performance.
Recognition and rewards: Recognize and reward your team members for their achievements and contributions.
Performance management: Hold your team members accountable for their performance and take corrective action when necessary.
Communication: Maintain open lines of communication with your team members to ensure that everyone is on the same page and working towards the same goals.

Conclusion

Managing a sales team requires a combination of leadership, communication, and sales expertise. By building a strong sales team, setting clear goals and metrics, and motivating and managing your team effectively, you can achieve your sales objectives and drive business success.

Chapter 6: Sales and Marketing Alignment

In today's business environment, sales and marketing alignment is critical to driving growth and achieving business success. In this chapter, we will explore the importance of sales and marketing alignment and the techniques used to achieve it.

The Importance of Sales and Marketing Alignment

Sales and marketing alignment is the process of aligning the goals, strategies, and tactics of your sales and marketing teams to achieve your business objectives. Alignment helps to break down silos between sales and marketing, improve communication and collaboration, and ensure that both teams are working towards the same goals. Some key benefits of sales and marketing alignment include:

Improved lead quality: By aligning your sales and marketing efforts, you can ensure that your marketing campaigns are generating high-quality leads that are more likely to convert into paying customers.

Increased revenue: Alignment helps to create a more efficient and effective sales process, which can lead to increased revenue and business growth.

Better customer experiences: Alignment helps to ensure that your sales and marketing efforts are consistent and aligned with your customers' needs and expectations.

Improved data tracking: By aligning your sales and marketing efforts, you can improve your data tracking and analysis, which can help you identify opportunities for improvement and make data-driven decisions.

Techniques for Achieving Sales and Marketing Alignment

Achieving sales and marketing alignment requires a strategic approach and a commitment to collaboration and communication. Some effective techniques for achieving alignment include:

Defining buyer personas: Define your ideal customers and create buyer personas that both your sales and marketing teams can use as a reference point.

Establishing a shared language: Create a shared language and set of definitions for key sales and marketing terms to ensure that both teams are on the same page.

Aligning messaging and content: Ensure that your sales and marketing messaging and content are consistent and aligned with your buyer personas.

Developing a shared lead scoring process: Develop a shared lead scoring process to ensure that your sales and marketing teams are prioritizing the same leads.

Creating shared goals and metrics: Create shared goals and metrics that both your sales and marketing teams can work towards and measure their progress against.

Regular communication and collaboration: Encourage regular communication and collaboration between your sales and marketing teams to ensure that everyone is working together towards the same goals.

Conclusion

Sales and marketing alignment is critical to achieving business success in today's competitive marketplace. By aligning your sales and marketing efforts, you can improve lead quality, increase revenue, enhance customer experiences, and improve your data tracking and analysis. To achieve alignment, it's important to take a strategic approach and implement techniques such as defining buyer personas, establishing a shared language, aligning messaging and content, developing a shared lead scoring process, creating shared goals and metrics, and encouraging regular communication and collaboration.

Chapter 7: Sales Technology and Automation

The sales process can be time-consuming and complex, requiring sales teams to juggle multiple tasks and responsibilities simultaneously. Fortunately, sales technology and automation can help streamline the sales process, reduce manual tasks, and improve efficiency. In this chapter, we will explore the benefits of sales technology and automation, the different types of tools available, and how to choose the right ones for your business.

The Benefits of Sales Technology and Automation

Sales technology and automation offer a range of benefits for sales teams, including:

Improved efficiency: By automating routine tasks such as data entry and lead nurturing, sales teams can reduce the time and effort required to complete them.
Increased productivity: Automation can help sales teams prioritize their tasks and focus on high-value activities, such as closing deals and building relationships.
Enhanced accuracy: Automation tools can help eliminate human error and ensure that data and processes are consistently accurate.
Better data management: Sales technology can help sales teams manage and analyze large volumes of data, providing insights into customer behavior, preferences, and buying patterns.
Improved collaboration: Sales technology can facilitate collaboration between sales teams, enabling them to work together more effectively and share information more easily.

Types of Sales Technology and Automation

There are a wide variety of sales technology and automation tools available, each designed to address specific needs and challenges within the sales process. Some common types of sales technology and automation include:

Customer relationship management (CRM) software: CRM software helps sales teams manage customer interactions, track sales leads, and monitor performance metrics.

Sales automation tools: Sales automation tools automate routine tasks such as data entry, lead nurturing, and follow-up emails.

Sales enablement platforms: Sales enablement platforms provide sales teams with the content, tools, and resources they need to close deals and improve performance.

Predictive analytics tools: Predictive analytics tools use data analysis and modeling to predict future trends and outcomes, helping sales teams make more informed decisions.

Virtual selling tools: Virtual selling tools enable sales teams to connect with customers remotely, using video conferencing, chatbots, and other technologies.

Choosing the Right Sales Technology and Automation Tools

Choosing the right sales technology and automation tools can be challenging, as there are many options available, and each tool has its strengths and limitations. To choose the right tools for your business, consider the following factors:

Your sales process: Consider your sales process and identify the areas where automation can provide the greatest benefits.

Your budget: Determine how much you can afford to invest in sales technology and automation tools, and choose tools that offer the best value for your money.

Integration: Choose tools that can integrate with your existing systems and processes, to avoid duplicating efforts and causing confusion.

Scalability: Choose tools that can grow and evolve with your business, to avoid having to switch to new tools as your needs change.

User-friendliness: Choose tools that are easy to use and require minimal training, to minimize disruption and ensure adoption by your sales teams.

Conclusion

Sales technology and automation can provide significant benefits for sales teams, including improved efficiency, productivity, accuracy, data management, and collaboration. There are a wide variety of sales technology and automation tools available, each designed to address specific needs and challenges within the sales process. To choose the right tools for your business, consider factors such as your sales process, budget, integration, scalability, and user-friendliness. With the right sales technology and automation tools in place, your sales team can work more efficiently and effectively, driving growth and achieving business success.

Chapter 8: Continual Learning and Improvement

The world of sales is constantly evolving, and sales professionals must continually adapt and improve to remain competitive. Continual learning and improvement are essential for success in sales, enabling sales teams to stay up-to-date with industry trends, develop new skills, and improve their performance. In this chapter, we will explore the importance of continual learning and improvement in sales, the different ways to learn and improve, and strategies for implementing a culture of continuous learning in your sales team.

The Importance of Continual Learning and Improvement

Continual learning and improvement are critical in sales for several reasons:

Keeping up with industry trends: Sales professionals must stay up-to-date with the latest industry trends, including changes in customer behavior, competitor activity, and new technologies.
Developing new skills: Sales professionals must continually develop new skills to stay competitive, including communication, negotiation, and technical skills.
Improving performance: Continual learning and improvement can help sales professionals improve their performance, increase sales, and drive business growth.
Building relationships: Sales professionals who are knowledgeable and continually improving can build stronger relationships with customers, becoming trusted advisors and partners.

Ways to Learn and Improve

There are many ways for sales professionals to learn and improve, including:

Formal training: Formal training programs, such as courses, seminars, and workshops, can provide sales professionals with in-depth knowledge and practical skills.
Informal learning: Informal learning, such as reading industry publications, attending industry events, and networking with other professionals, can provide valuable insights and ideas.
Coaching and mentorship: Coaching and mentorship programs can provide sales professionals with personalized guidance and support, helping them identify areas for improvement and develop strategies for success.

On-the-job learning: Sales professionals can learn through experience, taking on new challenges and learning from their successes and failures.

E-learning: Online learning platforms and courses can provide sales professionals with flexible, self-paced learning opportunities.

Implementing a Culture of Continuous Learning

To establish a culture of continuous learning in your sales team, consider the following strategies:

Set expectations: Communicate the importance of continual learning and improvement to your sales team, and set expectations for ongoing learning and development.

Provide resources: Provide your sales team with the resources they need to learn and improve, such as access to training programs, coaching and mentorship, and e-learning platforms.

Encourage experimentation: Encourage your sales team to experiment with new ideas and approaches, and provide opportunities for them to try new things.

Recognize and reward success: Recognize and reward sales professionals who demonstrate a commitment to learning and improvement, and celebrate their successes.

Lead by example: Set an example for your sales team by investing in your own learning and development, and demonstrating a commitment to continual improvement.

Conclusion

Continual learning and improvement are essential for success in sales, enabling sales professionals to stay up-to-date with industry trends, develop new skills, and improve their performance. There are many ways for sales professionals to learn and improve, including formal and informal training, coaching and mentorship, on-the-job learning, and e-learning. To establish a culture of continuous learning in your sales team, set expectations, provide resources, encourage experimentation, recognize and reward success, and lead by example. With a commitment to continual learning and improvement, your sales team can stay competitive and achieve long-term success.

Chapter 9: Conclusion

Throughout this book, we have explored the fundamentals of selling, prospecting and lead generation, closing sales, managing sales teams, sales and marketing alignment, sales technology and automation, and continual learning and improvement. We have discussed the importance of each of these areas and provided strategies and tips for success in sales.

To recap, the key takeaways for success in sales include:

Developing a strong sales mindset, including persistence, optimism, and resilience. Focusing on the customer and understanding their needs and preferences. Building strong relationships with customers, becoming a trusted advisor and partner. Embracing technology and automation to streamline sales processes and improve efficiency. Continuously learning and improving, staying up-to-date with industry trends and developing new skills. To be successful in sales, it is also essential to have a positive attitude, excellent communication skills, and a willingness to adapt to changing circumstances.

In conclusion, success in sales requires hard work, dedication, and a commitment to ongoing learning and improvement. Sales professionals must continuously adapt to changing customer needs and preferences, embrace new technologies and tools, and develop new skills to stay competitive. With a focus on the customer, a commitment to learning and improvement, and a willingness to embrace change, sales professionals can achieve long-term success in the dynamic and ever-changing world of sales.

As the world of sales continues to evolve, it is important for sales professionals to stay up-to-date with the latest trends and technologies. In the future, we can expect to see further advancements in sales technology and automation, as well as a continued focus on the customer experience. By staying on top of these trends and embracing new technologies and tools, sales professionals can continue to thrive in the years to come.

We hope this book has provided you with valuable insights and strategies for success in sales. Remember, success in sales is achievable for anyone with the right mindset, skills, and dedication. With a focus on continuous learning and improvement, you can achieve your goals and succeed in the exciting and rewarding world of sales.

Appendix: Additional Resources for Success in Sales

To further support your journey towards success in sales, we have compiled a list of additional resources and tools that can help you develop your skills and stay up-to-date with the latest trends and strategies.

Sales Blogs: Check out popular sales blogs such as SalesHacker, SalesGravy, and HubSpot Sales Blog for articles, tips, and insights from industry experts.

Sales Podcasts: Listen to sales podcasts like The Sales Evangelist, The Advanced Selling Podcast, and The Salesman Podcast for expert interviews and sales advice.

Sales Books: There are many great sales books out there, but some of our favorites include "The Challenger Sale" by Brent Adamson and Matthew Dixon, "Spin Selling" by Neil Rackham, and "The Psychology of Selling" by Brian Tracy.

Sales Training: Consider enrolling in sales training courses, such as those offered by SalesGym or Sales Readiness Group, to develop your skills and stay up-to-date with the latest sales techniques and best practices.

Sales Conferences: Attend industry conferences such as Sales Enablement Society Conference, Sales 3.0 Conference, and Inbound to network with other sales professionals and learn from experts in the field.

Sales Technology: Stay up-to-date with the latest sales technology and tools by regularly checking websites such as G2 Crowd, Capterra, and SalesTech Star.

Remember, there is always room for improvement and growth in the field of sales. Continuously seeking out new resources and tools can help you stay ahead of the competition and achieve your goals.

EXCLUSIVE PAPERBACK CLOSES

Assumptive closes and more about what they are

Assumptive closes are a sales technique used to assume the customer has already made the decision to buy and to close the sale by presenting the customer with a statement or question that assumes they are going to make the purchase. Here are some examples of assumptive closes:

1. "So, would you like us to schedule a delivery for next week?"
2. "Shall I go ahead and process the payment for you?"
3. "When would you like to schedule your first service appointment?"
4. "Let me get your paperwork started, can you confirm your address for delivery?"
5. "Great, so it sounds like this is the right product for you. When would you like to take delivery?"

These statements are designed to assume the customer has already made the decision to buy and to move the conversation towards the next steps in the sales process, such as scheduling delivery or processing the payment. Assumptive closes can be an effective technique to close a sale, but should be used carefully to avoid coming across as pushy or aggressive.

Trial closes and more about them

Trial closes are a sales technique used to gauge the customer's interest and to assess how close they are to making a purchase decision. Trial closes are usually open-ended questions that allow the salesperson to gather information about the customer's needs and preferences, and to provide feedback and recommendations based on that information. Here are some examples of trial closes:

1. "What do you think so far?"
2. "How do you feel about this product/service?"
3. "Can you see this product/service meeting your needs?"
4. "Do you have any questions or concerns that I can address?"
5. "How do you envision using this product/service in your business/life?"

These questions are designed to encourage the customer to share their thoughts and feelings about the product or service, and to provide the salesperson with an opportunity to address any objections or concerns that the customer may have. Trial closes can also help the salesperson to identify additional needs or preferences that the customer may have, which can be used to make further recommendations and close the sale.

Urgency closes and more about them

Urgency closes are a sales technique used to create a sense of urgency in the customer's mind, and to encourage them to make a purchase decision quickly. Urgency closes are usually statements or questions that emphasize the limited availability of a product or service, or the importance of taking action quickly to avoid missing out on an opportunity. Here are some examples of urgency closes:

1. "This is our last unit in stock, so if you want it, you'll need to act quickly."
2. "Our current promotion ends at the end of the day, so you'll need to decide soon if you want to take advantage of it."
3. "Other customers are interested in this product/service, and it may not be available for long."
4. "Our inventory is moving fast, and we can't guarantee that we'll have this product/service available for much longer."
5. "This is a limited-time offer, and if you don't act now, you may miss out on this opportunity."

These statements are designed to create a sense of urgency in the customer's mind, and to encourage them to make a purchase decision quickly. Urgency closes can be an effective technique to close a sale, but should be used carefully to avoid coming across as manipulative or pushy.

Direct closes and more about them

Direct closes are a sales technique used to ask for a purchase decision directly and explicitly. Direct closes are usually short and to the point, and leave little room for ambiguity or hesitation. Here are some examples of direct closes:

1. "So, would you like to purchase this product/service today?"
2. "Are you ready to move forward with this purchase?"
3. "Can I put this product/service on your order now?"
4. "Shall I process the payment for this product/service?"
5. "Would you like to buy this product/service now, or do you need some time to think it over?"

These statements are designed to ask for a purchase decision directly and to remove any potential barriers or objections that the customer may have. Direct closes can be an effective technique to close a sale, especially if the salesperson has already built a strong relationship with the customer and the customer is highly interested in the product or service. However, direct closes should be used with care to avoid coming across as pushy or aggressive.

Alternative closes and more about them

Alternative closes are a sales technique used to present the customer with a choice between two options, both of which involve making a purchase. Alternative closes are usually phrased as a question that presents two options for the customer to choose from. Here are some examples of alternative closes:

1. "Would you prefer to go with option A or option B?"
2. "Is it the blue or the red model that you would like to purchase?"
3. "Do you prefer to pay in full or take advantage of our financing options?"
4. "Would you like to take delivery today, or would you prefer us to schedule it for a later date?"
5. "Which option works best for you, buying the product outright or leasing it?"

These statements are designed to give the customer a sense of control and involvement in the sales process by presenting them with a choice between two options, both of which involve making a purchase. Alternative closes can be an effective technique to close a sale, especially if the customer is struggling to make a decision between two options. However, alternative closes should be used carefully to avoid making the customer feel pressured or forced into making a decision.

Thank you for taking the time to read "Mastering the Art of Sales: Strategies and Techniques for Success in a Dynamic World." I hope that this book has provided you with valuable insights and strategies for achieving long-term success in the challenging and rewarding world of sales.

I believe that sales is an art that requires both skill and dedication, and that anyone can become a successful sales professional with the right mindset, knowledge, and techniques. I hope that the strategies and techniques outlined in this book will help you to develop your skills and achieve your goals in the field of sales.

I would like to express my gratitude to all of the sales professionals who generously shared their knowledge and insights with me during the writing of this book. Their expertise and experience have been invaluable in shaping the content of this book and ensuring its relevance to the field of sales today.

Once again, thank you for choosing "Mastering the Art of Sales" as your guide to success in sales. I wish you all the best in your sales career and look forward to hearing about your future successes.